Breaking Up Is Hard To Do

Author, singer, and songwriter, Sue Coleman, proudly presents her debut book and album, *Breaking Up Is Hard To Do*. She resides in New York City. Sue would love to hear from readers. Visit her website at www.colemansue.com or follow her on Twitter @thesuecoleman.

Breaking Up Is Hard To Do

Sue Coleman

Biographical Publishing Company
Prospect, Connecticut

BREAKING UP IS HARD TO DO
Copyright © Sue Coleman 2015
All rights reserved.

Published by Biographical Publishing

Edited by Andrea M. Pilsner

ISBN 9780991352135

Printed in the United States of America

Music Credits:

Sue Coleman – vocals
Josh Lattanzi – guitar, bass
(backup vocals track 1)
Jason Roberts – guitar, bass
Pete Remm – keyboards
Greg Wieczorek – drums & percussion
Tyra Juliette – backup vocals
(all tracks except 1 & 11)

All songs produced by Josh Lattanzi

Recorded at
Degraw Sound, Brooklyn, NY
(engineered by Josh Lattanzi, Ben Rice)
Mercy Studios, NY, NY; Walk-Up, NY, NY
(engineered by Josh Lattanzi)

Mixed by Ben Rice at Degraw Sound
Mastered by Fred Kevorkian at Kevorkian Mastering, NY, NY
Book and album design by Bob Jones, Bob Jones Design, NY, NY

All songs written by Sue Coleman
© ℗ 2015 Sue Coleman
All rights reserved.

www.colemansue.com

❖ ❖ ❖

To my beautiful mother, Anne, who has read
this book and listened to these songs a million times.

I love you, Mom.

❖ ❖ ❖

Table of Contents

Author's Note

This book was written for a female audience and written from a woman's perspective. I refer to some of my experiences with men as examples to describe certain loser characteristics, although women can easily possess the same traits. I trust that you will be able to see in specific areas throughout this book, the differences between men and women, which can lead to the cause and effect of some undesirable relationships. I try to be fair in expressing that the world would be a better place if women would act like ladies and men would act like gentlemen, because when both behaviors are neglected, both sexes suffer.

There is something in this book for everyone: those who are seeking a relationship, those who are not, and those who are somewhere in between. I would like to highlight one important reason why this book was written with a female audience in mind. Back in the good old days, women would get married off at the age of 18, have children, and start a family. Today, whether you wish to have a career or not, if you don't get out there and work, you'll wind up destitute. Times may have changed but one thing hasn't, the stigma attached to a woman who is not in a relationship. I feel it is a modern day curse regardless of what you are seeking. If she does not have a man, so to speak, the fact that it may be by choice is a preposterous notion and she is most likely considered to be desperately seeking one. Women are perceived as untruthful, strange, man-haters, or they must have some deep rooted daddy issues if they say that they're not interested in having a relationship.

If men aren't in a relationship people assume that it is exactly where they choose to be and can even appear macho if they're life-long bachelors, while women would be considered spinsters. I am in no way suggesting that women should desire to be alone their entire lives but I want to point out that this stigma can make us feel as if the relationship box always needs to be checked. This can be a huge impediment throughout our lives and lead to a roller coaster ride of disconcerting relationships.

This stigma can cause confusion and conflict within ourselves if we deeply desire something more. Constant demands and distractions can take over from trying to fill this so-called mandatory void. We aren't sitting at home waiting for Mr. Right to take care of us. We're out there working our butts off. When I hear people say you should be able to make time for a career and a relationship, my response is, you should live a day in my life and tell me how much time and energy you have left over.

The people who do make it work and who are content were fortunate to have found a supportive, compatible partner. This may take a lifetime for someone else. Unfortunately, the majority of society looks at what other people have and they feel entitled to it. People try to fit in and live up to the standard of having it all. This mentality is unhealthy and it is almost impossible to lead a happy life this way. We each have our own purpose, which comes with our own struggles and triumphs. Some may find true love early in their life and some may find it later on. Some may lose it and never find it again or it may look like some have found it but they really haven't. You never know what may be around the corner but in the meantime you could be something extraordinary waiting to happen and may never know it if you're too busy trying to fit in and live your life according to other people's standards.

Preface

Can't live with someone—can't live without them? It may be a figure of speech, but truly feeling this way can literally tear you apart inside. I felt compelled to write this book not only to help people end and avoid bad relationships, but also as a reminder to embrace your life in whatever phase it may be in. Especially, during your single years which should be considered as one of the greatest times of freedom and self-discovery.

I've grown to become more thankful for each day of my life, which has led me to view who I let into it as a serious responsibility. Life may have its ups and downs and some of it may be out of our control, but it's also a sum of all of the choices we make. Who we let get close to us is a choice. Sometimes people may fool us, but sometimes we let them for various reasons. I've reached the point where it is no longer acceptable to waste time with people who do not deserve to be in my life. Taking the time to get to know someone is essential to avoid winding up playing the fool whether you know it or not. Not knowing what you have until it's gone is a rough lesson to learn and one in which I've been fortunate enough to have only imagined the consequences before it was too late. My main intention and the driving force behind completing this project is for you to have the same outcome. Now I think of each day as great considering what would have been if I had remained in some of my dead-end relationships.

I try to get to the point quickly and speak from my heart creating an easy read, which can be read in one sitting and again and again when needed. Leading off is the lengthiest chapter, Sex Rule, as it sets forth the foundation for the subsequent chapters. As for the accompanying album, music has always energized and helped me bounce back and move on after a break up. When the idea of *Breaking Up Is Hard To Do* surfaced, I knew I had to incorporate my songs into it. I wrote them long before this project emerged and that's the beauty of it—the songs genuinely have their own back-story. After writing the book draft and completing the heart of what I was trying to convey, the relevant songs were then chosen for each chapter. I believe the outcome is a unique benefit, in that it adds more meaning to the lyrics and in turn enhances the chapter's message and essence, increasing the chances of having a lasting positive impact.

Introduction

Nobody longs to be with a loser but sometimes it's hard to break free from one or avoid getting involved with one in the first place. It may seem like all of the good men in the world are married or have a girlfriend. This may be true, but it doesn't mean that you should settle for someone who constantly disappoints you.

It may seem harsh that I use the word loser to describe a person, but for the purpose of this book and actually helping people, I think it's the best word to get my point across. Throughout, I will describe loser characteristics that will ultimately cause you heartache. This does not mean this person is an overall loser, maybe in the ways of the world they are very successful, which does not matter in regards to loser relationships or in other words, *doomed to fail* relationships. Keep in mind the main focus here is on the aspect of how someone treats *you*, how it will affect *your* well-being, *your* life, and *your* overall purpose in it.

The chapters to follow contain simple rules for the vulnerable times in your life, whether you're young, mature, rich, or poor. The intention is for the reader to take them into consideration as a whole. By the end of the book my hope is that your outlook on relationships, love, and life will lead you into a happy, healthy direction. It's also intended to be referenced at times in the future when you may unexpectedly need it the most. Keep in mind that some of these rules and the supporting topics may seem like common knowledge but to live by them takes courage, strength, and willpower. I believe it can gravely affect your life if you do not. Choosing to be alone for a while or to endure unacceptable behavior should be a no-brainer but many women are ashamed to be alone, when in fact, they should be ashamed to let someone treat them badly. This game of life can cause us to experience some unpleasant things such as: fear, loss and unfulfilled dreams. This can lead to all sorts of addictions. Oftentimes getting involved with the wrong person and remaining in a loser relationship is not viewed as an addiction but it should be.

The topics discussed in each chapter are based on experiences that I've lived through and observed in the lives of people close to me and in society. The conclusion in all of these instances is that people don't change. I've learned that lesson through experience, but realize that a lot of people have not. It is difficult for human beings to change even when they desperately want to. Fixing or changing another person is something that would be a never-ending task of heartache. Some people hope and believe that by marrying someone, it will miraculously change a person into what they need them to be but in reality the unbearable flaws will only be magnified.

The idea of marriage and the excitement of a proposal can blind someone to the fact that they are rushing into making a lifelong commitment to someone they do not really know. In some instances, marriage and children are looked at as a goal that must be attained in a certain time frame. Settling or making hasty decisions may seem appropriate. This book is not intended to break up marriages especially when children are involved. It is intended to help single people end bad relationships and ultimately avoid marrying the wrong person or marrying for the wrong reasons. I point out and give some reasons for what may lead us to and why we would continue to endure certain types of relationships that commonly lead to failure and cause harm.

I hope you enjoy the accompanying album. These songs have stories of heartbreak and of picking yourself back up when it seems impossible—a song can help when you need a good cry or a good laugh, and to ease the pain when people can't. These songs were chosen for each specific chapter to shed some light on it and bring it to life. Each chapter ends with a lyric and relevant song name for your reference. The last song "Long Gone" does not pertain to a specific chapter. It's a reminder that to miss loving someone is part of the process of breaking up and it may not be the actual person you are missing. Longing to love someone can stir up some overwhelming emotions especially when your mind adds the pressure of society, friends, and family. These are the times to acknowledge your vulnerability, remind yourself to be extra careful, and to stay strong. This is when you may be inclined to let your guard down and let the wrong person in.

#1

Sex Rule

Sex is a powerful drug. People can get addicted to it and never love or care for the person they are sleeping with. It can also be the fuel that ignites and keeps the flames of a toxic relationship burning. The old saying, "saved the best for last" does not apply to this chapter. I started with the most important rule to abide by: ***Don't have sex until you get to know, like, and become real friends with someone.*** The word friend is often used too lightly. I'd like to point out that real friends should be interpreted as having a mutual love, respect, and trust for each other. It may be 101, but awful or undesirable relationships and unwanted pregnancies can be avoided if you get to know someone before getting addicted to sex with them out of lust, loneliness, or if you're in some rebellious stage in your life. Get to the root of your problems. Maybe you're simply looking for love and after a few dates you believe you've found it. Well, it takes a lot more than a few dates to truly get to know someone.

Sex with a stranger may feel good temporarily and you may have amazing chemistry, but eventually, you may wind up with someone who you don't even like and who you cannot tolerate. If you do get pregnant by a person like that, can you imagine the rest of your life?—not so much fun anymore. If you decide to have an abortion, well, that's not such a good feeling either. How many times will you roll the dice and risk getting a disease? Having sex right away and getting into a relationship without knowing someone is one of the reasons why people cheat on each other. God forbid we take the time to get to know someone. People often wear many masks and can put on quite the charade to hide their actual disposition and motives. Pay close attention to any subtle clues that make you feel as though something is not quite right. Let nothing get by you and do not ignore that which you do not wish to endure.

You may know someone who didn't take the

time to get to know a person, had sex right away, and now they are living happily ever after. Good for them but I'd say the chances of that happening are slim and there are a lot of loser frogs out there who will never turn into prince charming. Sooner or later a person's true colors will come out and when they do, you're already in it and it may be very difficult to cut them off. Great chemistry is essential but most likely not enough unless the rule above goes along with it. A chemical reaction to someone can feel as if a love spell has been a cast upon you. When reality sets in, it feels more like temporary insanity.

Some situations may not be so innocent. Someone may know right away that they're going to play with another's emotions until they've had their fill. Sex shouldn't be used to toy with or get what you want out of someone or as a form of self-validation. Not only is it mean and wrong—it's dangerous. I've heard stories from my men friends who would try to figure out women who were just not very nice people. There are some men who will get hurt, brush it off, and move on. There are a lot of nut jobs out there today who could snap in an instant if you play with their affections. Even if you start out with the upper hand, you can still lose—don't gamble on people.

This goes for both sexes but men have the ability to physically overpower us and we should never forget that.

There are some people who decide to move in together soon after they start having sex but without knowing each other well enough. I don't believe people should live together until they get married but I understand why they would be inclined to do it. I am not condemning it. However, it is not a wise decision to force or rush into these move in situations. It's hard enough to get out of a relationship when intolerable behavior starts to slowly present itself but now your living alongside it, going to sleep with it, and waking up to it—it's a huge difference. Moving out is not as easy as it is to move in, especially if one of you does not want to go.

Do not mistake moving in with someone and becoming their f*ck buddy as getting to know, like, and becoming real friends with them. Sometimes people move in together out of convenience and sex becomes a part of the situation. Feelings may get lopsided. The relationship is based solely on sex. You cannot force someone to love you. Whether you're living together or not, these casual friends with benefits relationships will eventually grate on your self-confidence and integrity. They will unconsciously wear you down. I tried having a casual relationship in order to avoid any more emotional turmoil after breaking up with someone and started to see a man who was in a similar situation. We had great chemistry and were always excited to see each other. However, I knew that he was not the type of guy who I would ever consider getting serious with. At the time, it seemed like a perfect situation to protect myself from getting hurt again while maintaining my newfound freedom.

Eventually, I realized I wasn't able to continue to have a superficial relationship. My mind would not allow me to do that to myself. Essentially, some of these situations may initially seem more than what they are if you're inexperienced or if you're on the rebound, but either way you're cutting yourself short—this could damage your self-esteem in the long run.

Alcohol consumption was definitely a contributor in accelerating and prolonging my casual affair. It's important to be sober in order to see things for what they really are, because you eventually will. Sometimes casual relationships can feel like 50 first dates, it always feels new, fun, and exciting. It's easy to get swept away when your perception of reality is distorted if you're both drinking every time you go out. You have to ask yourself, have I ever spent any time with this person without drinking? If the answer is no, you should try to do something that involves no alcohol.

Be careful in play it safe or on-again/off-again relationships, where nothing is really wrong, but nothing is really right either. It's somewhere in between—the main aspect is that you can go long periods of time without seeing one another. I continued to have various kinds of relationships like this through the years and it wasn't until I fell in love again that I acknowledged the fact that I was playing it safe the whole time. I am lucky to have lived through all of them without any ramifications. I've observed similar situations in the lives of other people who were not so lucky. Be careful with these types of relationships as they usually end up poorly.

If you can stand to be away from a person for so long, then you probably cannot endure to be around them for too long either. The part to be wary of is as time turns into years and your living your own life and the other person is living theirs, you may feel as if you have some special connection because you've known each other for so long. Maybe you're thinking it's time to settle down. You start to fear the future and there's no one else around. You compare them to other people who have disappointed you. This makes them seem more wonderful.

But how well do you know them? If you added up all the time you've spent with them, how much would it be? I've seen a lot of people in these situations where they keep a person on the back burner for years until they're ready to get married and one day wake up thinking who the hell did I marry. If two people really love each other, they're not going to let years go by uncommitted knowing there's a chance someone else may scoop them up. Some people may disagree and believe that you don't need to be head over heels in love, but that may be because they never were and don't realize what they are missing. They may end up settling or not leave themselves open to a more meaningful relationship.

If you do decide to wait or you have been waiting a long time for the right person to fall in love with, you'll begin to make a list of how many bullets you've dodged and how much time would have been wasted, not to mention, lost dignity and respect for yourself. There will be plenty of men along the way who will not wait to have sex with you. Good. They'll make it easy for you to find out what their sole interest is and you won't have to bother with someone who doesn't believe you're worth the time. Some men may wait but insult or pressure you along the way. Some men will be pleased you made them wait. My advice is to always go with the latter. Some people have told me they've waited and it wasn't worth the wait. Yes, I agree that will definitely happen, but I bet there were other things going on that made them realize this person was not for them. They decided to have sex with the person anyway. I've done that, and have regretted going against my instincts, but never regretted getting to know someone. The point is, in the instances where the sex is worth the wait, but the person is not, you'll have seen the truth before the effects of sexual dependency in an abusive, bad, or toxic relationship have taken a hold. Knowing the truth beforehand makes a huge difference in having the strength to say goodbye. For me, it has been difficult in both. I know that the difference of getting to know someone first has saved me from possibly living in a trailer park, barefoot and pregnant, as opposed to the very happy life I lead now.

You may say, "I want a casual relationship". Really? With someone who is out doing half the town? Deep down inside, I doubt that is what you want, unless you're out doing half the town too; then I'd say you're living life dangerously and it's time to grow up. Take a good look at how you're living your life to determine which category you may fall into: A) Someone who is emotionally mature, truly ready, and wants a committed relationship, or B) Someone who believes they are ready, but in actuality only wants certain aspects of a relationship.

When you know you are ready for a serious relationship, it's very important to recognize when others are not and when they fall into category B. If someone isn't ready to commit, they will eventually want out.

If you fall into category B, you may not be ready to commit to a relationship and that's okay. It's acknowledging that, which can save years of confusion and conflict if you're constantly in and out of unsatisfying relationships. Reasons for not being ready for a commitment can vary: underlying fears and insecurities to a preference of focusing your time and energy on something more important to you. It could also simply be that you're a free spirit by nature. The reasons do not always have to be something negative or psychoanalyzed—just by being consciously aware and admitting what you want or do not want, will help you close the revolving door of loser relationships. If you conclude that you're harboring some emotional issues, try to identify their origin through research. But once you pinpoint them, don't label yourself—learn, discover, and move on. There are siblings who have lived through the same traumatic experience, one may be fine and the other may not. What sets them apart is: their mindset, their character, their nature. Their experience will only define them if they let it—a victim mindset will not help you. Seeking out a psychologist may be helpful if you find a good one. I tried going to one for a while and learned one important thing about myself that I found very useful, which in hindsight made the rest of the sessions worthwhile.

If you've moved in with someone and the sexual bliss has ended and it turned out to be a mistake, but now you've become dependent on someone or vice versa, it doesn't mean that you should remain there. Try to save two–three months rent, look in the classified ads for the cheapest roommate deal that you can find. If it's your place, look for a roommate for them if you're reluctant to just kick them out. It may be uncomfortable for a while but desperate times call for desperate measures. Once you have succeeded in putting an end to this relationship, do not have sex with your ex under any circumstances. There's a reason that it came to an end. Remember that reason.

As for avoiding the whole moving out drama in the first place, wait two–three years before moving in with or marrying someone. There are no guaranties for anything in this world but if something is right, then you have nothing to lose by waiting. You will only be gaining by waiting—more is more in this case. The real person will emerge. It will help you find out if it's headed in the wrong direction and if sex or other factors were masking any underlying problems. A biological clock ticking or financial woes should not dictate your acceptance of a proposal. Think about the person and sincerely recite out loud the wedding vows that you will be making to them before you get swept away in the idea of marriage and all of the festivities that go along with it. "I _____ take you, _____ for my lawful wedded wife/husband to have and to hold, from this day forward, for better, for worse, for richer, for poorer, in sickness and health, until death do us part." If you choke on any part of them, it may be a good indication that you're marrying the wrong person or for the wrong reasons.

I feel that age has made me better, smarter and I truly know myself now. I am more focused and there is a sense of peace that I did not have before. I now know the type of people I want in my life. I don't want to say to wait until you're a certain age to get married but make sure you are at peace with yourself before you commit to it and that any future prospects are as well. Getting out in the world, meeting, dating, and getting to know various people will give you a broader sense of who is out there and will help in determining if someone is right for you. You don't need to sleep with all of these people to figure that out. To take the pressure off of dating scenarios, find joy in the actual experience of spending time with another person. If you approach each date expecting or hoping for marriage material, you're setting yourself up for disappointment. I've met, gone out with, and dated quite a variety of men. It has helped me know exactly what I don't like or want.

One of the hardest things to let go of is remembering and missing having sex with the person who you broke up with. If the sex wasn't that good it probably won't be that difficult, but if it's the mind-blowing kind, you may think that you'll never find someone who can make you feel the way that person did again. The following suggestion to help get over this and not fall back into the sex trap, may seem adolescent, but don't knock it until you try it. Watch as many movies as you can with your favorite movie star—the one with massive sex appeal who oozes sexuality and confidence. The one who makes you forget that there are any other men out there when watching him. You may never meet these stars in your lifetime, but who cares, it can give you hope that there are other men who possess the manliness you crave. Giving your mind this charismatic someone else to watch and think about may be a temporary fantasy but it will definitely help in the withdrawal phase. Romance novels work just as well or even better. Using your own imagination can have a stronger hold and impact over your focus.

Whether you like to consume alcohol or not, the following is important because there is always a first time for everything and drinking seems to be a common source of healing that people turn to after a break up. Evenings filled with alcohol can be the accelerator of a top-notch loser relationship, especially if you're on the rebound. For the nights when you'd like to blame promiscuity on alcohol consumption, try eating a lot more and drinking a lot less. Sounds too simple? It can really be that simple if a conscious effort is made. I know at times it is easier said than done so try playing the following role, it may change your perspective. Just for fun, make believe you're a reporter on assignment and go out to a venue where you like to have a good time and don't drink any alcohol. Drink club soda, let people think that you're drinking, blend in, and have a good time. Then observe what all the drunk Casanovas look like when you're sober and try not to forget. Here's a warning of what you may encounter. One night I started dancing with a guy which lasted less than one minute and this was the entire conversation—nothing more, nothing less.

Guy dances like a fool. I try to keep a straight face while bopping my head.

Guy: Do you live in the city?

Me: Yes.

Guy: Do you have an apartment?

Me: Yes.

Five seconds later . . . as guy continues to dance like a fool.

Guy: I wanna go to bed. Let's go to bed. I wanna go to bed.

Me: Sorry, you're not my type.

Guy walks away.

  I couldn't have made that up if I tried. You may

be thinking, even if you had too much to drink, you wouldn't give a fool like that the time of day. True indeed, but when you are drinking, encountering fools like this can make everyone else seem more appealing even when they are not.

If you're out on a date, don't be afraid to eat and make sure that you've eaten enough throughout the day. Drink water as your main beverage, with a cocktail in between. You will thank yourself in the morning if you pace yourself, know your drink limit, and don't go beyond it. It may seem like someone has your back because you're out on a date, but most likely they want to get you on your back and the more liquored up you are, the closer they think they are to getting what they want. If you're thinking that the whole point of drinking is to be drunk enough for when you wind up in said position, then you need to reread this chapter.

These suggestions may sound absurd as considering them would stifle your sex and social life, having fun is what life is all about. Unfortunately, sometimes our idea of fun can lead to bad consequences. It's all about your mindset beforehand. Once you have made it up to get intoxicated, you're consciously setting up a situation for the alcohol to take the blame and not yourself. We are the ones in control of picking up the glass and consuming the alcohol. Listen to that little voice inside your head, even though it may be spinning. Listen to what it's asking you. Should I have another? If it gets to this point, it's not too late—this should be your cue to go home (alone).

Action Summary

Stand up for what you want. Say what you want when you want it. Don't let anyone talk you into something to please them. Start thinking of yourself as a queen, a princess and if someone doesn't like it—well, isn't that just too bad.

Four Martinis
"Four martinis under your belt, trust me honey, love is not what you felt . . ."

2

Liar Rule

When someone tells a little white lie, I'm not going to say to completely write them off if there is good reason, like not hurting your feelings, but if someone tells you a lie right away, it could be an indication that they may do this on a regular basis. I was in a relationship with a pathological liar and it was not pretty. I cried every day until finally I caught him in a lie that he was unable to worm his way out of. It was a vulnerable time in my life and I felt as if I could not live without him. I constantly tried to leave but he was relentless in changing my mind. The truth was buried somewhere under all the gifts he bought to appease me. I lived in denial and would see what I wanted to see because I was desperate to break free but not strong enough to do it. When I look back, I do believe we had a rare connection, but there is no reason on this earth that could ever justify the knots I felt in the pit of my stomach every day. If it were not for my mother, I would have married this man, had his children, and then would have jumped off the Brooklyn Bridge.

A lot of my girlfriends have put up with lies and I find it disturbing. They make excuses and are willing to settle and waste endless hours talking about someone who is an untrustworthy snake. If I had told them this rule: ***Don't ever fall in love with a liar and if you already have, stop living a lie***, they probably would have said it doesn't pertain to their relationship. It's a scary thing to face reality, look at someone one day, and then realize that you've been with a stranger the whole time. I am older now and pray I've learned my lesson and never get involved with a liar again. That's why I must always get to know someone before getting lost in lust, which may turn into love. Otherwise, you're one of those girls who people shake their heads at and wonder what on earth has possessed her to endure such deception.

It's pretty easy to tell when someone is lying. They may start out by not keeping their word with simple things. Let's say a guy asks if he can take you to dinner one night and asks for your number and if he can call you later that evening. He never calls and then sends you a text a few days later asking you if you're free for the weekend. You respond, "yes." He then proceeds with his invitation, "we should meet for coffee or tea." That is not flat out lying, but not keeping your word is shady and lame. If something came up, that's a different story, but that was not the case. I actually encountered a guy like this and I responded, "I don't do coffee or tea, what happened to dinner?" He replied, "dinner is cool", then I never heard back until a few days later, when he texted "hello". Of course, I did not respond. I guess he was hoping I'd forget. A lot of people forget. This is really just letting things go and acting polite when it comes to this texting BS. Texting is a nice shield for people to hide behind when they want to do things their way and not be called out on it.

Liars make good cheaters and the two go hand in hand. "Oh, where were you, babe? Nowhere, just having sex with one of the girls from work." Imagine! They have to come up with a nice little cocktail of lies to account for their tawdry affair. Usually this will involve calling their friends to make sure they have an alibi, which makes you think they must be telling the truth. How could all of these people (his friends) possibly be lying to you? Believe me, I've seen it, and when it comes to covering for their buddies, they do it in a heartbeat. They think it's a big joke and that's what you'll feel like if you ever find out.

It may seem like someone loves you and there is no reason for them to cheat on you. This may be true, but there are some people who cannot commit to one person and love the thrill of doing something wrong and getting away with it. This book is intended to find you before you make the mistake of marrying this kind of person but I thought it important to share the following story involving a newlywed couple. A guy married a young, beautiful girl and right away he bought an apartment for his girlfriend who he had on the side (and occasionally other girls when it was party time). He supposedly loved his new wife but obviously did not want to give up this life of debauchery.

What bothers me the most about lying cheaters is how they put another person's health at risk without a second thought—especially when they've taken a vow to love, honor, and cherish. Then they have the audacity to lie, cheat, and risk passing on a disease. I'm sure there were signs that this man was a liar or something to give his wife a clue. Maybe she ignored the signs. Sometimes being with a wealthy person makes people see what they want to see. It's important to keep in mind that marriage doesn't cure lying and most likely will turn out to be a license for the liar to do it even more.

When you're getting to know someone, do not be afraid to ask questions. I used to feel as if I was being nosy but I realized that it isn't an imposition, it's necessary. If you're genuinely interested in someone there should be a natural exchange. You don't want to seem like an interrogator but asking questions here and there is not a crime. If the person makes you feel as if you're committing one, you should be wary. If the person is a liar, these questions can help you find out sooner rather than later, as oftentimes their answers conflict within another conversation.

If you are in a relationship with a liar, get out. Your heart will be broken but living with a broken spirit is much worse. If you think they will change, you are wrong. I doubt you will ever be able to trust this person. Trust is the most important aspect of a relationship. If you think that you can have a healthy one without it, you're sadly mistaken.

There are all sorts of con artists in the world and some happen to be charismatic womanizers who will charm the pants off of you. You may fall in love with one or find yourself heading in that direction one day. They may treat you like gold and catching them in a lie may never happen. However, recognize when things don't add up which is bound to happen when you're with a phony. They could be amateurs, making it easy for you to pick up on their lies or they could be experts, but even pros make mistakes.

When getting to know someone, especially if it seems too good to be true, observe how they interact with the rest of the world: how they treat their friends and family, how and why their past relationships ended, their work ethic, and business dealings. If you notice some questionable behavior in any of these areas, don't believe you are the chosen one and they couldn't possibly treat you the same way. It's only a matter of time until they do or until you find out. If you decide to ignore any chilling discoveries because you're deeply in love and your heart is set on making it work, remember that love is not enough sometimes. If you become seriously involved with a two-faced person who engages in crooked dealings, you will unknowingly and inevitably become a part of them.

Unfortunately, the life you lead and the things you've acquired in it, may be their next target and the main prize in their eyes.

Note the following applies throughout wherever the words get out or end it are mentioned:

It is extremely difficult to do just that if you're with someone who won't let you go. So once you've gone through the motions of talking out the situation to death (letting them down easy) and it's officially over (in your mind), don't pick up the phone and if you feel they may try to see you against your will, change your normal routine. If you must get or give back belongings, make sure some time has passed after the break up and have more than one person accompany you during the exchange. Also, ending it doesn't mean calling this person or answering their call because you're lonely or you miss them as time goes by. When it's over, it's over.

I did not write a chapter that addresses physical abuse, because in my perspective and I hope in everyone else's, that it is not to be tolerated under any circumstances. However, I recognize the importance of mentioning it here as it gravely pertains to this get out or end it note. If you've decided to end a relationship and the thought of following through causes you to fear for your safety, I strongly urge you to seek professional help and involve law enforcement.

Action Summary

To avoid getting involved with a liar, look out for little things that are said and then not followed through on. It could be you catching them in a lie right away—little or big. Call them out on it right away. Demand to know why they told you the lie, which will open up a dialogue to uncover their real motives and character. There's no need to be polite if you feel you're being lied to. What have you got to lose except the stress of being deceived? They may have a great story. If you're not convinced, don't let the liar continue the dance. Stop playing the music and leave.

In Love with Danger
"I love those eyes, I hate goodbyes, not as much as you tellin' me lies . . ."

#3

Manipulation Rule

We have all been or eventually will get manipulated, especially when we're young. There is a part of us that knows we are being manipulated—our conscience. Likely, we'll ignore or make excuses for this behavior because there is something that fascinates us about our manipulator. They tend to give us a great sense of pleasure, excitement, romance, and security. *Listen to your conscience—it's the voice of God and always knows best.* Listen to the people in your life who care about your interests. They are the ones who will be telling you what you do not want to hear. You can deny–deny–deny and pretend that it's all okay, but if all you do is cry–cry–cry, this is not love.

They love you. So what? In their own way they may but who wants to be in love with a fraud? You could certainly find plenty of psychological answers in co-dependency textbooks, but here's my take. I could have incorporated manipulation and lying into the same chapter, but after experiencing both your average liar and your master manipulator, I thought it best to keep them separate. I chose to highlight the sole reason why you would endure certain manipulators—they are usually masters at the art of seduction. Yes, lying and manipulation go hand in hand but the seduction is the main tactic to be wary of. The result is a dangerous love/hate game that you can get caught up in quickly, especially when paired with vulnerability.

If you're seeking an escape route from life's stressors, the drama that this manipulation creates can make you feel alive. Deep inside the lack of something important may feel as if it's slowly killing you. If you're already suffering and facing that reality is too much to bear, it makes sense why you might choose to play the fool. Enduring this pleasure/pain game replaces your true source of agony and provides a gratifying, exciting component. You may grow to love this person, but the foundation of that love is built on a big, fat lie. It will come crumbling down when you're finally willing to open up your eyes and see the light. This is similar to many of life's addictions but it's viewed differently and seems to get a free pass because it revolves around the idea of love. If you are the manipulator: When manipulation dies out and you're left face to face with the other person, they will eventually see you for who and what you are. The fantasyland will not last and will always come to an end. I promise.

There is another less severe and more common form of manipulation. Insecure guys will pursue someone they like by playing adolescent games. They do not have the guts to court you the way they know they should and the way a real man would. You may entertain these games out of boredom or out of your own sense of control. Letting these types of relationships play out can lead you to develop feelings for a guy who doesn't have much of a backbone. Confident, real men are a dying breed. Where have they all gone? Women today are the aggressors. Stop and let men go back to being men.

When you endure men who do not possess confidence and then find one who does, it's as if you've found the king of the earth. If it turns out they are not worthy of a crown, you may be inclined to stay because you don't want let go of the illusion of strength that initially pulled you in. Confident men are hard to come by and I believe women are starving for them. Good news, you will eventually find one. Bad news, it may take a while before you find a good one with genuine self-confidence.

Do what you have to do even though it's going to hurt like hell. When you're going through the motions, it's important to focus on all the things that you can no longer live with and not what you think that you're unable to live without. I've always believed in the 21 days to acquire a habit/get rid of one myth. This is not to say that getting over someone will take 21 days but remember that the beginning of the end is the most difficult part. It won't always hurt that bad—it will take time but little by little the pain will subside.

Keep in mind that manipulators know too well the effect they have on you. They will try to see you to talk it out. Staying in their presence will only prolong your torment. If possible, all closure conversations should be spoken over the phone. The beginning of the end is the most crucial time to stick to your decision, right after you've made it. It may be easier if they let you go without a fight. If they don't, success may be quite a struggle. To help you succeed, I suggest taking a trip to a place where there are things to keep your mind busy and yourself far away from them. Your trip information should not be disclosed to them and all forms of communication with them should be cut off. Upon your return, if they are persistent or seeing them is unavoidable (e.g., you both take the same train to work); you will be stronger since some time has passed. Even if it's only a little, it may be all you need to break you out of the trance you were in. Throughout this time, they will likely continue their arsenal of tactics causing you to second guess yourself. Keep that in mind when reading the following chapter with respect to self-esteem. It will be needed to break free from manipulation.

I've heard people say that they try to seek out the good in people. That's nice but when someone sparks your interest don't put them on a pedestal until they've proven that they deserve to be there.

Action Summary

There are various degrees of manipulation. To determine if it is the serious kind, ask yourself if it impacts your entire relationship. Constant manipulation is a problem that must be addressed. The point is, you can only deny something temporarily and eventually you'll come to your senses (if you have any left; you may be numb at this point). Don't be a denial zombie. Get out of this relationship before it's too late. Avoid suffering any permanent damage this person's manipulation could have on your life.

Sometimes

"Sometimes love's not enough, you gotta leave and no one's there to touch. Sometimes you wish he was here, can't wish upon a star when reality's too clear . . ."

#4

Offensive Rule

One of the best ways to identify a loser is if they offend you. Blatant or subtle, it doesn't matter. The fact that they're insulting you and hurting your feelings is not right. If something someone says makes you feel bad and insecure, it probably wasn't by accident. Most of the time people are jealous or have their own inferiority complex—neither of which is your fault or your problem. ***Don't even attempt to try to fix offensive people or try to be perfect for them.*** Friends and lovers should love and support you. If you're enduring envy, criticism, possessive behavior or verbal abuse—this is not love or support. There are enough things in this world to keep you down. When it comes to the people in your life, at least you have the choice to get rid of them or not befriend them in the first place. You may be alone, so what. It's an old saying but it is better to be alone than in bad company.

Keep in mind that offensive behavior in relationships is also a control tactic used out of the offender's own fear of losing you. They might feel threatened by your interests and pursuits which may lead them to mock and discredit your efforts. It's important to know what you want and do not want out of your life. Knowing what you do not want can be enough to save yourself from becoming one of those people who molds into whatever the other person prefers them to be.

In certain areas of our lives it is unavoidable, such as the workplace. On a daily basis you may have to endure people who thrive on being annoying. The only way to stand up for yourself is to give them a taste of their own medicine by telling them off (like a lady of course). Insult them back and it shuts them up. After that, they always want to be your best friend. Most often, the best thing you can do is ignore and distance yourself from these people.

There are many beautiful people in the world who never realize how beautiful they really are—

inside and out. Sometimes they focus on the smallest thing that keeps them from loving who they are. Learning to love yourself and becoming your own best friend is necessary to successfully lead a happy, healthy life. In order to accomplish this, you must forgive yourself for anything that you feel guilty about or makes you feel unworthy. You may discover things that you'll need to do in order to make yourself a better person, but work on them and you will. When you've become your own best friend, you will not succumb to an offensive person's nonsense. Being happy with yourself and loving yourself is a prerequisite to being able to love and make someone else happy. Sometimes you may encounter someone who is good for you, but the timing may be off. You may need to get to know yourself better, iron out some of your rough edges, and grow up before being able to make a relationship work.

A great way to get rid of negativity and stress is by exercising, which you'll especially need after a break up to keep your mind and body strong. Even if you are the one who ends it, you will be vulnerable. It's important to get dressed and ready every day because when you look good you'll feel good. Even if you only get ready to go out and take a walk, it will lift your spirits. Walking is one of the healthiest things you can do for yourself on a daily basis. Letting yourself go will make the process of moving on twice as hard. Don't turn your back on the person who needs you the most—yourself.

Taking care of yourself should be an enjoyable, essential part of life. You don't have to spend a fortune on gyms, salons, and spas. There are a plethora of remedies and exercises that you can do at home if you're pressed for time and on a budget. When I come home from a stressful workday, if I take a bath and pamper myself, I feel like a queen. Treat yourself like royalty and you'll begin to feel that way.

The following may not be the answer to it all, but it can help unearth your inner goddess and help you to discover amazing qualities you may not have known you possessed. Schedule a professional photo shoot with a hairstylist and make-up artist—the whole works. Be sure to do some research to find a legitimate photographer. Personally, I take much better pictures with female photographers. When your beauty is maximized and seen from a different perspective, your self-confidence will grow as lovely aspects of yourself come out of hiding. If you take pictures, there may be many unflattering ones, but that is what the delete button is for after you've determined your good side. Usually, the best pictures will come toward the end of the session when you're relaxed and enjoying it.

I recommend removing something from your life that makes you feel secure on the outside. Not necessarily on a permanent basis but so you dig a little deeper on the inside. Here is an example of what I mean. For over two years, sneakers were the only shoe that I was able to wear due to an injury. Any other type of shoe would cause my knee bones to grind against each other. I went from feeling glamorous to feeling like a limping little nothing, among other things. I noticed a lot of women would stare at my feet. I felt like I was constantly being judged. Even after I explained my problem, they'd forget and comment on the way I dressed and would ask me, "Why do you always wear sneakers? You would look so pretty in a dress." As if I had never worn a dress before or knew how good I would look in one.

I was a friggin' actress. Every day was Halloween, so you can imagine my frustration. I wanted to scream, not only at all of these people, but how everything I had worked so hard for seemed to vanish because of this injury. Now I had to worry about pleasing the fashion police. Surprisingly, when I would go out, men would approach me more than when I used to dress up. I think I seemed more down to earth, literally and figuratively. Heels had given me a false sense of security and not being able to wear them helped me to rediscover my true self-confidence. The physical pain forced me to relax and stay home a lot, which left me no choice but to deal with what was going on inside myself. It felt as if I had been stripped of my identity. As a result, I discovered things that I had never imagined. It brought a new dream to life after an old one had died. The heavens have a way of working their magic, even though it may come in the form of misery.

At times it may feel as if your ego is trapped inside a piñata and people are constantly taking turns trying to knock it down. Don't worry about getting those pieces back, let 'em have them. Just don't let it eat at you. Forgive them and move on. Say a prayer for them and wish them well. Cry if you need to— don't hold it all inside. Then use that negativity and your battle scars in a positive way. Let it motivate you into doing something profound for yourself and share it with others. Life isn't about being perfect, nobody is. You just need to be you—imperfections and all. Nobody can take that away from you.

It's easy for me to tell you to cry but in case you have trouble expressing your feelings, the following is important. Do you ever wake up and cannot figure out what is bothering you? Or you go to sleep that way? Sometimes we run away from our emotions and aren't even aware that we're doing it. Learning how to breathe deeply and meditate is a great way to get in touch with what's going on inside. Keeping a daily journal will help you run toward your feelings and not away from them. When I was younger I discovered how bad this problem was for me during my theatrical studies which turned out to be extremely therapeutic.

I'm not suggesting you become an actor but it may be helpful to research the types of classes that actors take to figure out what might work for you. The Alexander Technique and different types of meditation would be useful. They can be found on DVDs instead of taking an actual class. Some people may scoff at this suggestion. They believe they are who they are. They are set in their ways. Really, it's never too late to learn, especially when it comes to having peace of mind. My emotions run deep. At times they are quite overwhelming to deal with. Until

I did, they were an obstacle to unlocking my potential and being able to accomplish my goals.

Note in general throughout regarding going out, having fun, and meeting new people:

When you do go out, whether alone or with friends, do not measure a great time on whether you think you've met the one or not. I've found a lot of people to always be on the prowl and it to be their sole reason for going out. Meeting new people doesn't mean searching for the one, a hero, a savior, or whatever name your mind may be conjuring up. Watch the classic movie "Auntie Mame" with Rosalind Russell. She said it best, "Live! Life's a banquet and most poor suckers are starving to death!" Life was meant to live, even if you're going at it solo.

Action Summary

Spend some time alone. Find out what you're good at and what interests you. Take some classes accordingly. You need to relax and have fun, do the things that you enjoy either by yourself or with a good friend. Schedule an event at least once a month to have something to look forward to. Meet new and interesting people instead of staying with someone who makes you feel bad about yourself.

Haven't Lost My Fire

"When I wake up, splash water on my face, look in the mirror, I embrace . . . "

#5

Selfish Rule

Did you ever notice that if a man has a stressful, time-consuming job, the woman is usually supportive and accommodating to his schedule? In my experience, when it's the other way around—well it usually isn't, because you either put up with whining and manipulation, or it's just not worth putting up with. It seems like a man's ego cannot or does not want to understand how you can possibly stay away from their manliness. They want what they want, when they want it, and that's it.

I'm not saying don't make time for someone, but people (especially women) tend to forget their dreams when they're with someone. Unless that is what you honestly want, it will only lead to resentment down the road. You may be able to have both, but it can become impossible when you're with someone who is selfish. ***Don't get bullied into feeling or believing that your true passion should be put on hold because it's not as important as someone else's needs, wants, and desires.***

Selfish people can be cunning, envious, mean-spirited, and close-minded. They have issues which are not worth trying to uncover. They tend to be vengeful if your attention does not revolve around them. This nature can be one of the reasons for cheating which they will carry out as their way of revenge, especially if they feel you've sexually slighted them.

There are selfish people who can be defined as controlling or users. "What can you do for me?" is the constant narrative in their mind. If you receive the silent treatment, a guilt trip, and are walking on eggshells around these people if you don't cater to their needs, I can guarantee this is not a true friend. This goes for family members as well.

In order to save yourself a lifetime of heartache, do not even consider a serious relationship with this type of person. If you're already involved and you see a chance to escape, do so at your earliest opportunity. This may be a difficult and grave decision to make if you're at the beginning of what seems like a perfect relationship. You may be inclined to deal with it because you're still in that new blissful stage. Beware! When the glimpses of selfishness begin to overshadow the good, this will not be an easy life. You'll wind up feeling very alone. The only benefit of experiencing someone who is truly selfish is that you'll appreciate it when you find someone who isn't. It could turn out to be someone who you would not have considered giving a chance to before, but someone who deeply cares for you and your happiness.

If you're worried about losing controlling, user-type people as friends—stop worrying. You should be more concerned with how they will hold you back from your own life if you continue to waste precious time and energy trying to please them. It may feel as if you're losing a lot of friends, but you're actually finding out that is not what they were in the first place.

Note in general throughout regarding feeling as if you're losing your best friend:

The following may apply throughout, however, I put it under this chapter, because the selfish characteristic is not so black and white. It's something that you almost feel as if you're unable to debate, but one where the underlying issues this type of person can possess are quite disconcerting and sometimes revealed a little too late. Thus, you may be inclined to stay in the relationship when you feel as if you're losing your best friend. That said, I know the worst break ups are when you feel this way, it's almost as if you're grieving a death. It can be an extremely depressing time. However, I've had a lot of best friends throughout my life who didn't quite live up to the best or the friend part very well. If there's a reason that makes you know you have to let someone go, I'm sure they weren't living up to the true meaning either. What makes the situation even harder to follow through on, is feeling sorry for them when they come groveling back. I'm not saying do not forgive them, but they didn't feel bad when they were doing whatever they did to hurt you, so by staying strong and following through in ending the relationship, you may feel as if you are losing your best friend, but you are simultaneously becoming your own best friend in the process. In certain instances, you may have simply grown apart from your best friend, but in either case it's still going to be very difficult to let go.

Action Summary

Test people to find out if they truly care about your needs or if they are only concerned about pleasing themselves. It's not difficult to figure out if someone is selfish, they often have a pompous mentality. If you attempt to bring their flaws and hurtful actions to their attention—well, good luck with that. Don't let others chronically hurt or use you through expecting too much at your expense.

Here Come the Heartbreakers

"It takes a will of iron and a loaded gun to kill off these feelings, and then run far away cause you were not enough. It was you I loved . . ."

#6

Disrespectful Rule

Is it really that difficult for people to treat one another the way they want to be treated? Apparently so, at times it seems worse than ever. ***Respect yourself and have respect for other people.*** It seems like an epidemic today, especially in New York. More men than not are incredibly rude and disrespectful. The Internet and having venues advertised as "best hook-up places in NYC" has helped this new era of brutes. Who can blame them? I would like to but a lot of women, including myself, have allowed it in one way or another.

Do you remember the old-time movies and how the ladies and gentlemen behaved? That was not an act, the men back then treated women with respect and the women had dignity and respect for themselves. My grandfather was a real gentleman and I learned a lot from him. He used to point his finger at me and say, "Remember kid, nobody's better than you, doesn't mean you think you're better than anybody else, but nobody's better than you kid." You all remember that too (I'm pointing my finger at you). "Nobody's better than you kid! Nobody's better than you."

In today's world it may sound old-fashioned, but I expect to be treated like a lady when a man takes me out. I want to be fair and acknowledge that there are a lot of gold-diggers out there and can understand men being cautious. It's also true that many women are becoming the breadwinners. Men, especially younger men, are now looking for a sugar mama. There are a lot of lazy people. People who have had a hard life and they feel that everyone owes them something. This behavior is now easily blamed on the economy. Precious time and money can be saved by having, dare I say it—actual telephone conversations. I believe they are necessary to feel out someone's character and determine chemistry. I remember the days when I looked forward to speaking to someone on the phone. Now should I be grateful to receive a text? I don't think so.

Yes, I expect to be treated like a lady. If a guy takes me out to dinner, I expect him to pay for it. There are many men who feel that if they take you out, you owe them sex. One night, I had a date with a guy and we had some drinks and appetizers at a restaurant bar, which lasted about an hour. We didn't have an ounce of chemistry and weren't even flirting. Afterward, he asked me if I wanted to go to a hotel. I was highly insulted and told him off. He said, "Come on I just bought you dinner—you're gonna be like this?" I'm not saying a man is a loser or a bad person if he tries to sleep with you, but if he insults you because you won't sleep with him, this is behavior that you should not tolerate.

I wish for one day men were able to get pregnant. Men who had sex with random girls would take a pregnancy test and find out they were going to have a baby. Instead of life returning to normal for them, they could feel the horror of looking at the positive test result which would remain with them forever. I know you may think, well, just wear a condom. Would you have sex with someone who you knew had AIDS with a condom? The majority of people would not. There's always a risk. I know people who have used condoms and who have gotten pregnant. I also recall a time when a condom had been deliberately removed without my knowledge or consent. Women have to risk a lot more by having sex. It is beyond terrifying to think that you may be or actually are pregnant if that's not what you want. Men can pick up their pants and walk away. Yes, there are men who do the right thing and pay child support or take care of the child but there are a lot of men who do not. There are men who have children with many women and get away without taking responsibility for an unwanted pregnancy.

I started discussing unwanted pregnancies because that's a result of what can happen when sex is the only goal of men taking women out to dinner. If that goal is not met it's as if they lost out on some huge investment and want their money back. The bottom line is that women can make their own money and buy their own dinner. Men should be more than happy to take a woman out and be in her company, not that she owes her naked body in return. Do you think men ever stop to think about how much money you spend on getting ready for them? It is doubtful; they just expect you to look absolutely perfect.

After writing this chapter, I watched a news segment which discussed a study about picking up the bill at dinner in which 44% of men said they would dump a woman if she didn't offer to pay for dinner, even on the first date. I wish they would have countered that study with a woman's reaction and that 100% of women would have dumped the man if he expected that from her. If these particular men want the respect I'm sure they expect, then they need to act like men. What's next? Should a woman pull out the chair for them before they sit down and hold the door open for them?

The above may seem dated, as I've noticed a decline in men even asking a woman out to dinner. They'll just text you, hope and expect to have sex with you, and if not, on to the next in line. I feel sorry for the younger generation of girls who may think this is normal behavior. It is not normal. It is rude, cheap, and disrespectful. Quite frankly, it's pathetic and should not be accepted. I know it's hard for young girls today, especially when they feel in constant competition with each other. They are subjected to all sorts of mediums where women and celebrities who they admire are exploiting their sexuality. Sometimes it seems as if everyone is trying to prove how sexy they are. This is not something you should ever try to prove to yourself or anyone else, especially to someone who does not respect you. Keep in mind, you don't have to walk around half naked or get naked to show or prove that you are sexy.

The subtle things are what make a person alluring. It could be the way your eyes glow, your laugh, your voice, your kind soul, your sense of humor, or your intelligence. Keep your clothes on for a while. A little mystery goes a long way. I feel sorry for the younger generation of boys who do not realize that having sex with every girl in sight does not make them a man. Perhaps they could care less and will roll the dice and take their chances hoping to get lucky. They're setting themselves up for a shallow, careless lifestyle while missing out on getting to know someone who may be worthwhile.

Action Summary

The human body is a temple of God and nobody should put a price on it, including yourself. You don't have to look far for your power. It comes from within. You need to recognize how much you possess. Once you've discovered your power: embrace it, own it, and don't let anyone take it away from you by accepting their disrespectful behavior.

I Stand Alone

"Can't they see that I stand alone, this here woman, you cannot own . . ."

#7

Adultery Rule

I could have put this in with the first chapter, but I thought it was too important and should have its own rule. ***There are not any ifs, ands, or buts—stay away from married people.*** There's no good that will come from getting involved. Their spouse will always be haunting you. You will always wonder if you're the next victim. If someone is headed for divorce, let them get divorced but you better make sure that the real reason is not you.

If you find yourself in a situation where you are too attracted to someone but you need to be in their company or work purposes, either change your situation or do not give in. It may seem unfair or as if you have no control, but trust me, you have more control than you give yourself credit for. It may also seem as if you're not gaining anything by denying yourself this pleasure that you think you so deserve. Well, you're refraining from ruining your life and someone else's who does not deserve it. I know it can be quite a struggle to do the right thing. Developing a will of iron to go against what your body craves and desires is difficult. It's more difficult to live with the consequences of being tempted into doing what's wrong. When you succeed at overcoming moments of temptation and do the right thing, it gets easier and will become a part of your character.

You have the real winners (sic) who seek out married people because they see it as a challenge or are looking for some type of financial, sexual, or emotional benefit. This reason is unforgivable. This type of person needs to get a life of their own. I've witnessed women who have had no problem with going after another woman's boyfriend or husband. Some were self-confident who felt that they deserved whatever they could gain from it. Others were extremely insecure and it was as if they thought it made them seem more desirable and sexy if they were able to make a man cheat. Guess what? It never did.

A lot of men who are not seeking an extramarital affair but who may find themselves in a situation where they are attracted to someone, would not cheat if women didn't give them the go ahead. I believe that our bodies are wired differently and women bear more of the responsibility in these situations—if we would draw the line, men would not cross it. You may disagree, but if you were on the other side, you'd be thanking me.

It's important to keep in mind that the devil is constantly looking for ways to tempt you. It's not usually when you're at your strongest. He's very patient and will wait for your most vulnerable moments. The devil desires to go unrecognized in order to successfully carry out his work. We need to be aware and acknowledge that there is a force working against us, especially if we're going to beat it.

If you deliberately seek out married people and see it as a challenge, I seriously recommend that you seek help. You possess some deep-rooted issues. Your best bet is to pray and ask God to help you. Crying out loud or into a pillow and letting it all out to God is therapy in itself. Just be still and listen afterward to that small voice inside you. You most likely already know why you are the way you are. It's just a very uncomfortable feeling when you're face to face with yourself and there's nowhere to hide.

So the final note here is that there are enough headaches in life. I have more stories but the bottom line is you know you shouldn't be doing it. I don't have to tell you stories about murder to not have you kill someone. It should be the same way with adultery. Don't do it. End of story.

Action Summary

If you meet someone and the encounter leads you to believe that they have taken a personal interest in you, I would flat out ask if they are married or have a girlfriend before you give your number or get a number. If you feel that this approach is too forward, you shouldn't, it's necessary. Tell them you're into leading a drama-free life. You may not receive an honest answer but it will throw their game off course. It can help to figure out if something is not right. If you're lucky, they may not even bother contacting you once that question is out there. If you're not that lucky and find out they are involved with someone after a few dates, at least when you inquire why you weren't told—they cannot say you never asked. Be prepared for this type of answer: "I have one but we're kind of like roommates, we're really not in love anymore." Please do not give your number to this guy.

Don't Let Them Do You Wrong
"Keep your offer, I'm not interested, play me softer, I know how it ends . . ."

#8

Prayer Rule

There are people of many different backgrounds, faiths, and beliefs and it's difficult for anyone to say anything without offending someone, especially when it comes to religion. I felt compelled to say that I am not trying to promote religion by writing this chapter and want to briefly provide its intention. This is a self-help book based largely on personal experience so to leave out the most significant source of help that I have received throughout my life, especially in the areas that this book pertains to, would be pointless and untruthful. My faith and hope in God has given me purpose and the lack of it has miserably failed me. Working on this project has been a mentally, physically, and financially draining experience. If I did not feel that I was honoring God by completing and sharing it with the world, it simply would not exist. Even if the following does not coincide with your beliefs, I hope that it isn't overlooked. The content touches on the underlying importance of humility and not taking what you have in life for granted which tie together into leading a happy loser-free relationship life. Self-pity can provide justification for making poor choices in hard times.

Do you ever stop to think about all the things in your life you have to be thankful for without wishing for more? After surviving adversity, I have become grateful for everything I have. Some people are the opposite. They always have a why me attitude. All the hardship I've endured has only brought me closer to God. He is always there waiting for me to figure it out and has picked me up numerous times when I thought I had nothing left. At times I have felt abandoned, but I grew to realize that these unpleasant times were preparing and strengthening me for more important things that God has in store for me.

I'm going to elaborate on the above in case you're as stubborn as I am. I've been blessed having lived through complete helplessness and hopelessness only to have my situation completely turn around. It brought me to realize that God was waiting for me to truly turn to Him and surrender. I have lived through hardships, but until I experienced one particularly humbling time, I never understood how one could possibly give up their burdens to God. In the back of my mind it was probably my pride thinking that I was weak if I didn't do everything on my own. Some people, whether they've had it fairly easy or difficult, never discover how God works in their life. Some remain in their misery blaming everyone and everything, including God. Some float through life believing how wonderful they are without acknowledging God's presence and what He has done for them.

I complain and ask God for more when my anxiety gets the best of me. Old habits die hard but when I slow down and start each day by praying, meditating, and spending time with God it puts me back on track. I realize how foolish I've been thinking I can do it all on my own and I realize once again how much God loves me, wants me to lean on Him, and that I am not alone—none of us is alone. All of your trials, tribulations, rejections, failings, talents, gifts, and strengths—give them up to God and He will take them and make sure you're where you need to be through Him.

If you see a pattern of trusting and putting faith in people only to have them disappoint you, your relationship with God may need some attention. Sometimes we work so hard on a daily basis and it feels as if there's nothing to show for it. Life has its way of taking its toll on us and we may desperately want something real to see and touch. It seems as if God's love isn't enough. There are moments when God's grace is powerful and strong in our lives. We feel on top of the world. Other times His grace takes a vacation in order for us to suffer in silence, learn, and grow. During the times throughout our lives when we experience pain and suffering, the tendency may be to not pray or turn to God. Instead we may credit another person with qualities they don't possess in order to create our own idea of a hero in a desolate world.

Remember that God is always there for you, will never leave you, and is waiting for you to come back home to Him. Your relationship with God is something that should be your first priority. All your other relationships are gifts. Enjoy the time when you're alone. Embrace it. If and when the time is right, the right person will be there. Don't let a lifetime go by wishing upon a star. Live your life to the fullest. There are so many ways to do that by using the gifts you've been given. Don't ever let anyone tell you who you are or what you should be doing. Let God guide you and serve Him by what you know in your heart to be true. Have faith. Believe that there is a heaven above and that your life has a purpose. This will empower you to stay on the right track.

There are people of many faiths so I'm sure that there are many people who do not believe in or acknowledge the Blessed Mother. For those of you who do, it's important to say the rosary and pray to Her. If you're not familiar with the story of the Lady of Fatima, I urge you to read it. (The World Apostolate of Fatima, USA (www.wafusa.org) has a great publication: The Message of Fatima, Lucia Speaks.) I befriended a woman at work when offices were being renovated and was stationed next to her for a while. She taught me the importance of Mary and I am forever grateful. I began to say my rosaries and it helped me endure all that I happened to be going through. Our dear Lady has never abandoned my prayers and an immense sense of peace is always felt by Her presence.

Start each day by giving thanks and praise to God for all His love and everything He has given you. Call out a list of things you are thankful for. Especially after a bad break up or when you're life isn't going so well.

You'll begin to feel a lot less sorry for yourself and realize how worse things could always be.

Action Summary

Pray in good times and in bad. Schedule your time around God, not the other way around. Get to know Him. Calm your mind. Cast aside restless chatter and hear God. Be still. Listen and learn His will for you in tranquility.

Don't avoid praying because of fear or shame. It could be shame of admitting your sins, fear of feeling vulnerable, or it could be that you don't want to deal with the truth and feel the emotions that might surface when you pray.

Back Home to You
"Jesus, my love, stay always in my heart. For times I depart the way that I do, thanks for bringing me back home . . ."

#9

Go With Your Gut Rule

The majority of the previous chapters are the basis for which relationships to end, and which to avoid. They are meant to ring a bell in your mind. I did not intend to try to dehumanize you. Keep it in mind to always give someone the chance that you think they deserve, unless of course you feel they may be some kind of stalker or serial killer. There is a fine line in giving someone a chance when your gut is telling you to run for the hills.

Note that the following is said with caution:

Sometimes I'll let situations play out if I feel I was too quick to judge although my gut instinct is usually right on the money. I find that if someone possesses any of the loser characteristics described in these chapters, they are most likely guaranteed to disappoint me. Some of them have tried to change. Actually, they were just hiding their true colors which started to emerge when they felt that I was under their spell.

You may decide that it's okay to befriend untrustworthy people and not get involved romantically. However, it's easy to get caught up and start to develop feelings for someone, even though you knew they were a mistake from the get go, especially if they're determined to be with you. Temptation comes in many forms—you have to look out for people who may just be distractions or worse. *If and when you're unsure which way to go, go with your gut.* There are mistakes in life that we can learn from and there are mistakes that will change your life forever.

We all know many unimportant things and often neglect to pay attention to what is most important. We know better, but sometimes don't choose to be around people who make us better. Do you remember when you were young and your parents didn't want you hanging out with someone who was a bad influence on you? I think that should never be forgotten. It's so easy to be brought down by another person.

If someone's presence causes you to feel alarmed, this is not the kind of situation I recommend playing out. If you are on the fence about someone (who does not invoke fear in you), make believe they are on probation. There's nothing wrong with giving someone a chance to prove your gut instinct wrong, but when they don't, move on. Say goodbye.

If the person is not someone who you should get involved with, think of the situation as if the person were a real criminal. Someone who violates their probation would go back to jail, not back on the street to continue being a sweet little criminal. The person who you gave a chance to and failed can go back to their life and you can go back to yours without them in it. This all sounds so simple, but we all know when someone is exciting, fun, and attractive it requires a good amount of self-restraint to let go. Remember, trust needs to be earned. Don't let the simplicity of pleasure provide a free pass.

Distinguish when something is your gut instinct versus gravitating toward someone. Someone's energy can be powerful and irresistible. You may think you were destined to be together. Maybe you were destined to meet but it could be for reasons other than you think. The purpose could simply be to learn something from each other. If the person has major issues and the attraction is very strong, you may confuse the pull you have toward them as something more. This could cause you to try to help them. I believe this is never a good idea. Try to be a positive influence where you can. Becoming someone's savior will suck the life out of you even if you are doing it out of true compassion. Attraction can be a very persuasive force, but do not let it dictate your being. Recognize when something has run its course and when it's time to move on.

The following deals with ending it when you are in too deep. What follows is one of the most important messages to remember if you ever find yourself unable to make the move that you know must be made. You may recall that I've mentioned how fortunate I was in being able to end things unscathed.

Here's the reason why I had this result—when the signs were sent to me from the heavens above, it was as if I had been struck by lightning. I did not ignore these warning signs. I knew that if I didn't get out, a storm was a comin' and it felt like it was a do or die situation. The signs may come in alarming forms but usually in the form of bad things happening stemming directly from the person who needs to be removed from your life. The signs did not come from my gut; however, after receiving them, my gut knew that something worse would happen that could not be undone. These are the moments that will define your life. You have a choice. Don't choose the easy way, avoiding the pain of a break up. Choose the hard way. Choose the pain. Choose to go with your gut after the signs have invoked fear in you, let it sink in, feel it, use it—allow it to force you to do the right thing. If you choose the easy way and refuse to end it—life as you know it may take a turn for the worst and there may be no way back to what you had. If that is the outcome, you'll have no one to blame but yourself, which is the absolute worst pain of all.

Assuming you will find the strength to say goodbye to the person who you've been holding onto, don't be surprised and expect them to find a new victim in the blink of an eye. When I said to choose the pain—I meant it. You will gain a sense of peace that will make it worthwhile once the negative person is out of your life for good.

If you are apathetic and the thought of losing what you have doesn't provoke any fear in you because you feel you don't have anything to lose, I understand, I've been there. A black cloud was my constant companion for over a decade and I believed that some people were not meant to be happy. I thought suffering was my lot in life. Thank God I was very wrong. Life is a series of highs and lows. If you constantly feel down, you may think you weren't meant to be happy, as I once believed.

When I am now faced with a choice that depends on my willpower, I am able to find the strength because I know the pain won't last forever. Perseverance and willpower have become two dear friends of mine. They've never let me down. When I look back, I feel ashamed that I did not appreciate all of my good fortune, but I also know what it is like to be completely hopeless. I guaranty if you made a list you'd find some things you would be afraid to lose, but the first thing you need to do is find hope. Dream something up and let it impel you into a better future and end this bad relationship once and for all.

Choose to be with and befriend people in this world who you can trust, who share your values, people who lift you up and make you a better person! Remember that it is a choice and being selective is not shameful and does not make you a bad person.

Action Summary

Mistakes are a part of life but if the same ones are repeated, lessons are never learned. It's as if you're constantly getting left back in school—and nobody wants to get left back or behind. To avoid having regrets when looking back at your life, don't let the wrong people into it. Those who may hold you back and leave you behind. Practice paying attention and trusting your gut instinct. It is essential to avoid harmful people and situations.

Don't Waste Time

"Keep on rockin', keep on rollin', don't waste time. Keep on rockin, goin' your way and me goin' mine . . ."

#10

My Three Wishes

Wish #1—May you speak up and stand up for yourself in all your relationships.

Wish #2—Make a man pick up the phone and speak to you before you go out with him. Get to know him without text messaging. This texting has killed any intimacy that you used to be able to have by speaking to someone on the phone. Don't be afraid to ask for what you want. Some men aren't afraid to ask for sex after they've bought you an appetizer.

Try this: Before you give out your number, tell the guy if he expects to go out or to hang out then you expect him to pick up the phone and call you. You may not like this approach and prefer someone to initially feel out your schedule through texting before having them call. I know it definitely can be useful at times and you should use your judgment on the situation and the person. However, if you both have the time to have a texting conversation and type out what you want to say, especially with someone who you don't know, why can't you speak to each other?

I find the back and forth to be irritating. You may not, but you can learn a lot about a person by talking to them on the phone. Just for the record, there isn't anything cute about a grown man texting that he's laughing, "bahahahahah". Wouldn't you rather hear his laugh? A phone conversation is not such a ludicrous suggestion. If someone has taken a genuine interest in you and is not socially challenged, I am sure that they would actually prefer it.

Wish #3—May you find what makes you happy and live to the potential of your God-given destiny without letting the evil ways of the world sidetrack you.

The Afterward follows this last chapter with a brief, but powerful story relating to the avoiding aspect of this book which I hope stays with you. I'd like to leave off here on a final positive note relating to the ending aspect.

Just because someone has failed us doesn't mean that we didn't fall in love and I know how hard it is to end it, but that is exactly what you need to do. Cold Turkey. Try to do it as amicably as possible or seek professional help if you feel the situation calls for it. End it. There's no other alternative. I've done it and I'm still alive, well, and better than ever. I cringe at the thought of what my life would have been like if I had not been strong enough to end my bad relationships abruptly. You may cry uncontrollably, but so what? Eventually you'll stop. Heal for a while. Forgive them and more importantly, forgive yourself.

Keep a journal and write down each day what you're going through, which is not only therapeutic, but can lead to some great discoveries and ideas. When you're ready or even if you're not, go out and have a good time—laughter is the best medicine. Take a trip or make plans to do something entirely new. Go to new places, meet new people, and make new friends. Have fun. Be happy that you're alive and free. It's a process. You'll have good days and bad, but time will heal. Just don't wind up with another loser to replace the old. Deal with the pain. One day you'll wake up and see that person on the street and you'll wonder what you ever saw in him or maybe not, but you'll thank God that it's over, as you continue to travel down the road of endless possibilities.

Let's Not Care

"Let's not care, in a good way. Listen to the music, yeah — it's time to play . . ."

Afterward

After spending two years working on this project, thinking I had experienced the worst and could not be tempted into being with a harmful person, I met the ultimate narcissist and one of the most charming creatures I had ever encountered. The sexual chemistry and the desire this person provoked in me was something I had never felt before in my life. The attraction was so strong I literally could not sit still until I saw him again. All I wanted to do was kiss him and be near him.

On the first date I met Mr. Gentleman nice guy. On the second date, which was having him over to my apartment for dinner, which I knew was a mistake, I met Mr. Liar and a few other people. I discovered something that evening which caused us to fight and resulted in him not getting his way. If the night had progressed more smoothly, I might not have seen all of his personalities unfold so quickly right before my eyes. It was as if I was living out a Lifetime movie. The next night I met Mr. Manipulator when we spoke over the phone as I listened to him rant and rave and say a bunch of incoherent things to me, which were not true and made absolutely no sense. I knew he was trying to make me feel I had issues because he felt rejected, but the things he said made me question whether he was on drugs or was a mental case.

I am a strong, intelligent woman and the sickest thing is that even after knowing the worst, my mind and body still wanted to receive the initial excitement and pleasure this man provided. I knew it was not remotely love, but that did not matter. I felt as if I was a crack-head and he was crack. I prevailed. There was no way I was going to let this person sabotage all my hard work. I was a few weeks away from heading into the studio to record my album and all it took was two weeks for him to turn my life upside down and me into a basket case. But I will say this, if my life had not been full of an enormous workload and responsibility at that time, staying away from him would have been like trying to tame a tiger.

Not easy, to say the least. Now picture if there had been a few more weeks of intimate encounters. Even though I notice some unpleasant characteristics, I am in deep. I make excuses and deny what I know is true. It snowballs out of my control. I am under the control of someone else, who is not a very nice person. Then comes trying to please all of the personalities I discover along the way. No thank you! Ok, I digress, but you get my point. The bottom line is that I temporarily broke my own rules. I went against what I know and have learned from past experiences. It may sound as if I learned an awful lot by having him come over on the second date and maybe that is the way to go—well, I can assure you, it definitely was not. I knew this type of guy was trouble and it could have had some grave consequences, which I was fortunate to have escaped. This may not seem very serious as I am not disclosing all of the details, but trust me, that night scared the absolute hell out of me.

Here's what happened before I made the wrong choice of having him come over: My mind went into a frenzy of an adrenaline rush. I blocked out all that I knew was right and pretended that consequences did not exist. My mind was made up. I did not even want to speak to him on the phone the night before. I did not want to get to know him and find out anything that may have ruined the fantasy. Please remember the following if you find yourself in a similar position one day.

Stop. Breathe. Take a moment. Calm down. Think of some of the consequences that you do not wish to endure. Take another deep breath and say a prayer. Ask

God for the strength to do the right thing before you make the wrong decision and not after it's too late. I learned from this experience that no matter what your age or how much you know, it only takes one wrong person to sweep you off your feet and wreak havoc in your life. It may take years of staying on the right track and doing the right thing to reach your goals, but all it takes is one stupid choice to kiss it all goodbye.

May God bless you and be with you and may you acknowledge him in your moments of weakness and ask for strength before the deed is done. Your mind will not stand a chance once you've already decided to go against what you know is right, true, and toward what you feel you're being deprived of. These rules are not for the weak, develop your will and stay strong.

One small request . . .

If this book/music helps you in any way, please leave a review to spread the word to someone else who may benefit from reading this as well. Thank you in advance.

Sincerely,
Sue

Lyric Sheets

Four Martinis

Sex Rule

Pressin' up against you kissin' your neck
Just the way that you like it
Feels like you know him so well
Have another drink cause you already fell
In love with this one he's hot as hell

Chorus:
Four martinis
Under your belt
Trust me honey
Love
Is not what you felt
No it's not what you felt

You have never been kissed like this
Fate has brought you to his lips
Makes your ex look so lame
He stares at you with the look of love
Makes you feel like a real woman

Chorus

Sittin' there sober back at the bar
Looks like he's not sure who you are
Your face was fallin' off when you were lit
Thank God you didn't wake up next to him
Pray it's the last time you drink that gin

Chorus

In Love With Danger
#2
Liar Rule

I love those eyes
I hate goodbyes
Not as much as you tellin' me lies
You told me once you told me twice
Kept on goin' just blocked out knowin'

Chorus:
I don't know who you are
I don't know who you were
I fell in love with danger
I was sleepin' with a stranger

It hurt so much
When I heard
Your last lie the one you couldn't deny
I saw that evil in your eye
Screamed so loud it was the hardest cry

Chorus

I don't know who you are

You told me once you told me twice
Kept on goin' just blocked on knowin'

Chorus

I don't know who you are

Sometimes

#3

Manipulation Rule

Sometimes it seems so unfair
When it feels like your life is going nowhere
Sometimes you know
To quit your cryin' and just let it go

Doesn't seem so bad I finally feel like
I'm headed somewhere even though I am scared
I finally feel I'm headed somewhere

Chorus:
I wanna love someone
I wanna be someone
When your light shines through me
It isn't so hard to breath
I wanna make believe
I wanna be set free
When your light shines through me
It isn't so hard to breath

Sometimes love's not enough
You gotta leave and no one's there to touch
Sometimes you wish he was here
Can't wish upon a star when reality's too clear

Doesn't seem so bad I finally feel like
I'm headed somewhere even though I am scared
I finally feel I'm headed somewhere

Chorus

Today is the day I see
Today is the day I see
A fool. . .I wasn't meant to be

Chorus

Haven't Lost My Fire

#4
Offensive Rule

There's a rumor goin' round
I lost my fire
All used up
My look is so tired
When I wake up
Splash water on my face
Look in the mirror
I embrace

Think before you speak
Do you speak the truth
Or are you just a liar
With no damn proof

Chorus:
Liar liar
I haven't lost my fire
In fact I'm so hot
This smoke's risin' higher

New phases goin' round
Can be real scary
When friends let you down
You start gettin' weary
When I wake up
Thank God I'm me
I never understood those wannabes
I never understood their jealousy

Think before you speak
Do you speak the truth
Or are you just a liar
With no damn proof

Chorus

Here Come The Heartbreakers

#5

Selfish Rule

Oh you're one of those heartbreakers
So they say call me what you want
But my heart still aches
From lettin' you go and when I wake up
Tossed and turned
Lived and learned

Chorus:
Here come the heartbreakers
Getting it done
Here come the heartbreakers
Look out everyone

Bein' the breaker may seem fun
It takes a will of iron and a loaded gun
To kill off these feelings
And then run far away
Cause you were not enough
It was you I loved

Chorus

Getting it done
We're gonna make you come
To the point of no return
On the flames of desire
We all get burned

Chorus

I Stand Alone

#6
Disrespectful Rule

Be brave take me as I am
Uniqueness my strength and all
Respect that I am real
Without amendments

Finds good one
possess woman

Chorus:
Can't they see that I stand
Can't they see that I stand
Alone
Alone
This here woman
This here woman
You cannot own
You cannot own

Where is your self-esteem
I won't lower my being
Or go back in time
With no exceptions

Finds good one
possess woman

Chorus

Nah Nah Nah Nah Nah Nah
Nah Nah Nah Nah
Alone
Alone

Don't Let Them Do You Wrong

#7
Adultery Rule

You belong to another and I'm much stronger
Than all the girls you crossed before
I'm the daughter of a long lost soldier
And I don't care anymore
Keep your offer I'm not interested
Play me softer I know how it ends

You'll wake up with beastly pangs of guilt
Used up feelin' like your youth is gone

Chorus:
Don't let them don't let them don't let them
No don't let them do you wrong

You're drivin' to the brink not without one last drink
You can taste that air but can't break free
To defy is no option this carnal need
It seems unfair that you cannot breathe
You learned this dance don't you miss a step
The consequence of abused adrenaline

Will you wake up or stoned cold still
Is it too much bearin' the love that's gone

Chorus

You're uncomfortably cornered
Will you do it again do it again do it again

Will you wake up—is it too much
Don't let them don't let them don't let them
Will you wake up or stoned cold still
Is it too much bearin' the love that's gone

Chorus

Back Home To You

Prayer Rule

A long lost love affair
Like distant air
You once breathed in
Is no longer there
I try so hard
To find somethin' true
It's so easy
When I turn to you

Chorus:
I am not afraid
I am not alone
When I find my way
Back home

When I'm lost
Can't be found
My most stubborn days
Search all around
Try so hard
To be rescued
It's so easy
When I just love you

Chorus

Jesus my love
Stay always in my heart
For times I depart the way that I do
Thanks for bringing me back home

Chorus

To you

Don't Waste Time

#9
Go With Your Gut Rule

Look the other way
It's the least you can do
Just another day
Of bein' blue
Not crossin' the line
Just another day
Of you goin' your way
And of me goin' mine

Chorus:
Keep on rockin'
Keep on rollin'
Don't waste time
Keep on rockin'
Goin' your way
And me goin' mine

I never needed you
Can't help but feel like this
It may be real
And I may miss
You all of the time
There's just no way
I'll ever be one of those
Girls who's so blind

Chorus

Let's Not Care

#10
My Three Wishes

Oh my goodness
I'm bored to tears
I haven't had my kind of fun
In too many years
Times are changing
The end is near
No it can't be
It's just the beginning for me

Oh my goodness
The end is near

Chorus:
Let's not care in a good way (x2)
Listen to the music—Yeah
It's time to play (x3)

Forget about meaning
And all of your strife
Is not the time to worry about
The problems in your life
You may think it'll never be the same
When everything's gone
All that's left is sorrow and pain

Oh my goodness
So much to fear

Chorus

Don't look down
Don't look up
Look them straight in the eye
And don't give a. . .

Chorus

Long Gone

Long gone
Long gone
My love is long gone for you
Long gone
Long gone
My heart has faced that truth
Though my head can't understand
Why I still think of you

Chorus:
Long gone now I long
To love someone
The way that I
I loved you

Long gone
Long gone
My love is long gone for you
Long gone
Long gone
I don't cry the way I used to
Though this life despite my tries
It can still be so cruel

Chorus

The way that I
I loved you

I loved you

Acknowledgments

On The Book Side

Thank you Mom for absolutely everything. Thanks for your endless patience and support throughout this entire process. I couldn't have done it without you.

Thank you to Kathy Takats for referring me to John Guevin at Biographical Publishing and for your encouraging praise and enthusiasm. Your words meant a lot and stayed with me throughout when this project began to take its toll.

Thank you to Joan Pokorny for taking the time to work on my initial draft. It was a great help.

Thank you to Gina Love for your never-ending support and help, and for all your advice on how to simplify aspects of this project enabling me to hang onto whatever bit of sanity I had left.

In addition, thank you to John Guevin at Biographical Publishing for your guidance and work on publishing this book; Andrea Pilsner for doing such a great editing job; Bob Jones for your ideas and fabulous design work on the overall project; and Bruce Colfin for your legal expertise throughout this project.

On The Music Side

First and foremost, I'd like to thank Josh Lattanzi whose incredible talent and production of this entire album brought it to life. Without him, it simply would not have been possible.

Thank you to all the band members: Josh Lattanzi, Pete Remm, Jason Roberts and Greg Wieczorek for your unique talent and for getting the job done so quickly. It was an awesome experience watching you play—you are all amazing.

Thank you to Tyra Juliette for your beautiful background vocals and for getting the job done in such a short amount of time.

Thank you to Ben Rice for your excellent mixing work; Fred Kevorkian for your excellent mastering work and to both of you for your time and patience.

A special thanks to an outstanding vocal teacher and singer, Lucas Kane Hall who taught me how to sing and enjoy it. Thank you for all your help and patience.

And always, thank you God.